Wheels Are All Around

By JOwen

Library For All Ltd.

Library For All is an Australian not for profit organisation with a mission to make knowledge accessible to all via an innovative digital library solution. Visit us at libraryforall.org

Wheels Are All Around

First published 2023

Published by Library For All Ltd
Email: info@libraryforall.org
URL: libraryforall.org

Our Yarning logo design by Jason Lee, Bidjipidji Art

Original illustrations by Caitlyn McPherson

Wheels Are All Around
JOwen
ISBN: 978-1-922991-05-8
SKU03393

Wheels Are All Around

Train

Toy

Push

Ride

Fast

Car

Bus

Truck

Plane

You can use these questions to talk about this book with your family, friends and teachers.

What did you learn from this book?

Describe this book in one word. Funny? Scary? Colourful? Interesting?

How did this book make you feel when you finished reading it?

What was your favourite part of this book?

download our reader app
getlibraryforall.org

About the author

JOwen is from the Nurrunga/Ngarrindjeri Nations of South Australia. She was born in Adelaide and now lives in Broome, Western Australia. She loves the laughs and fun of family gatherings. As a child, her favourite book was *I Can Jump Puddles*.

Our Yarning

Want to discover more books from this collection? Our Yarning is a collection of books written by Aboriginal and Torres Strait Islander peoples across Australia.

We know that children learn better, and enjoy reading more, when they see themselves in the stories, characters and illustrations of the books they read.

To download the app, visit the Google Play Store on any Android device and search 'Our Yarning'.

www.ingramcontent.com/pod-product-compliance
Lightning Source LLC
Chambersburg PA
CBHW042349040426
42448CB00019B/3470